THE
LEO
ORACLE

THE LEO ORACLE

INSTANT ANSWERS FROM YOUR COSMIC SELF

STELLA FONTAINE

greenfinch

Introduction

Welcome to your zodiac oracle,
carefully crafted especially for
you Leo, and brimming with the
wisdom of the universe.

**Is there a tricky-to-answer question niggling at you
and you need an answer?**

Whenever you're unsure whether to say 'yes' or 'no',
whether to go back or to carry on, whether to trust
or to turn away, make some time for a personal
session with your very own oracle. Drawing on your
astrological profile, your zodiac oracle will guide
you in understanding, interpreting and answering
those burning questions that life throws your way.
Discovering your true path will become an
enlightening journey of self-actualization.

Humans have long cast their eyes heavenwards to seek answers from the universe. For millennia the sun, moon and stars have been our constant companions as they repeat their paths and patterns across the skies. We continue to turn to the cosmos for guidance, trusting in the deep and abiding wisdom of the universe as we strive for fulfilment, truth and understanding.

The most basic and familiar aspect of astrology draws on the twelve signs of the zodiac, each connected to a unique constellation as well as its own particular colours, numbers and characteristics. These twelve familiar signs are also known as the sun signs: Aries, Taurus, Gemini, Cancer, Leo, Virgo, Libra, Scorpio, Sagittarius, Capricorn, Aquarius and Pisces.

Aries · Taurus · Gemini · Cancer · Leo · Virgo

Libra · Scorpio · Sagittarius · Capricorn · Aquarius · Pisces

Each sign is associated with an element (fire, air, earth or water), and also carries a particular quality: cardinal (action-takers), fixed (steady and constant) and mutable (changeable and transformational). Beginning to understand these complex combinations, and to recognize the layered influences they bring to bear on your life, will unlock your own potential for personal insight, self-awareness and discovery.

In our data-flooded lives, now more than ever it can be difficult to know where to turn for guidance and advice. With your astrology oracle always by your side, navigating life's twists and turns will become a smoother, more mindful process. Harness the prescience of the stars and tune in to the resonance of your sun sign with this wisdom-packed guide that will lead you to greater self-knowledge and deeper confidence in the decisions you are making. Of course, not all questions are created equal; your unique character, your circumstances and the issues with which you find yourself confronted all add up to a conundrum unlike any other... but with your question in mind and your zodiac oracle in your hand, you're already halfway to the answer.

Leo

JULY 23 TO AUGUST 22

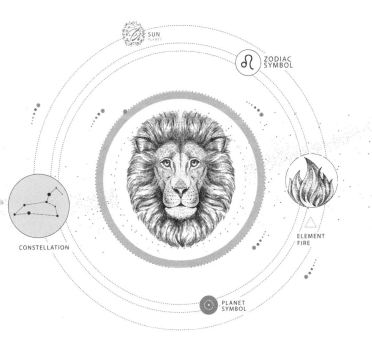

Element: Fire

Quality: Fixed

Named for the constellation: Leo (the lion)

Ruled by: Sun

Opposite: Aquarius

Characterized by: Generosity, warmth, leadership

Colours: Gold, orange, yellow

How to Use This Book

You can engage with your oracle whenever you need to but, for best results, create an atmosphere of calm and quiet, somewhere you will not be disturbed, making a place for yourself and your question to take priority. Whether this is a particular physical area you turn to in times of contemplation, or whether you need to fence off a dedicated space within yourself during your busy day, that all depends on you and your circumstances. Whichever you choose, it is essential that you actively put other thoughts and distractions to one side in order to concentrate upon the question you wish to answer.

Find a comfortable position, cradle this book lightly in your hands, close your eyes, centre yourself. Focus on the question you wish to ask. Set your intention gently and mindfully towards your desire to answer this question, to the exclusion of all other thoughts and mind-chatter. Allow all else to float softly away, as you remain quiet and still, gently watching the shape and form of the question you wish to address. Gently deepen and slow your breathing.

Tune in to the ancient resonance of your star sign, the vibrations of your surroundings, the beat of your heart and the flow of life and the universe moving in and around you. You are one with the universe.

Now simply press the book between your palms as you clearly and distinctly ask your question (whether aloud or in your head), then open it at any page. Open your eyes. Your advice will be revealed.

Read it carefully. Take your time turning this wisdom over in your mind, allowing your thoughts to surround it, to absorb it, flow with it, then to linger and settle where they will.

Remember, your oracle will not provide anything as blunt and brutal as a completely literal answer. That is not its role. Rather, you will be gently guided towards the truth you seek through your own consciousness, experience and understanding. And as a result, you will grow, learn and flourish.

Let's begin.

Close your eyes.

Hold the question you want
answered clearly in your mind.

Open your oracle to any page to
reveal your cosmic insight.

Hold onto your own self-belief Leo;
you have overcome many challenges
and experienced great personal
growth. You can handle this.

The depth of your real connections with loved ones should not be doubted Leo. Reassure them and yourself while you are at it. You have far to travel together.

You are a big personality Leo, charming and engaging and oh so likeable. Make the most of those very appealing traits now.

Celebrate your achievements Leo;

if you don't, then who will?

Although everything might feel like it is coming together beautifully, don't become complacent Leo. There are still things that could go wrong, but it will be easy enough to keep on track as long as you don't take your eye off the ball. Keep communication lines open.

Keeping productivity high and energy levels positive comes easier to you than to most Leo; your natural leadership talents shine through at times like this. Maintain the momentum and everyone involved will benefit.

Leo is the zodiac's
natural leader – powerfully
charismatic, seemingly unstoppable,
a super-friendly force to be reckoned
with. Just remember, some people
take longer to win over than others.

No one can fault your carefully measured, knowledgeable approach, but it might be that you are not giving this one the consideration it merits.

It is extremely tempting to stick
to the safe questions, but are you sure
this is really the one you want
answered? Try again.

Research time is never wasted
Leo, especially if you are looking for
an extra 'something' to push a project
or idea over the line to the next level.
Keep an open mind and soften your
focus to avoid tunnel vision.

Others sometimes see
your commitment to integrity
as unnecessarily self-important, but
it is essential if you want to maintain
everything you have worked
so hard for.

Your Leo nature rules supreme
and might be pushing you to put a
fair bit of pressure on yourself right
now. This one is tricky, but probably
not for the reasons you think.
Persevere and you'll do it.

Ease off on all those stretch-targets you keep setting yourself Leo, it's time to show yourself some love.

Your emotions have a way of running ahead of you Leo, and pulling you along with them. Be mindful and attentive to this possibility, as it can have a powerful effect and throw you off track if it sneaks up on you.

Be patient this time Leo; wise as you are, you are not all-seeing. There is still something you need to know.

The details are not precisely as they seemed at first glance. King of the jungle you might be, omnipotent you are not. Take a closer look – there is detail there that was not apparent to start with.

Making a difference is second nature to you Leo; with your natural talent for leadership taking centre stage at the moment, this is your time to really push your main points and help others find their own paths to success too.

If socializing options are abundant right now Leo, take the time to choose only those that feel meaningful and worthwhile to you. Your own enjoyment is important and stimulating company is key.

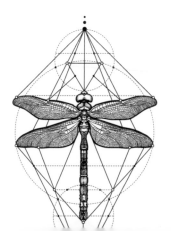

Clearing your head through physical activity, meditation or yoga, or connection with someone who understands you well, will help you to set your priorities in order and address this issue more rationally.

Relinquishing control may seem unnecessarily risky Leo, but it's time you learnt to believe in your star-path. The way ahead is already illuminated.

There is nothing you can do to plan for it, but you should know that change is on its way. Endeavour to remain open to the possibilities that lie ahead.

Hold your head up Leo, you can
be proud of how well-respected you
are becoming, and with good reason.
The opinions of petty-minded, jealous
people are not your concern – you
cannot control the feelings of others.

Success is coming, but it might be less spectacular than you had first hoped. A series of small wins is the key to this one.

Getting caught up with the buzz of what's going on is no bad thing Leo. See if there is something you can do to lend a hand and make a difference – getting involved is a great feeling.

Your Leo gifts for honesty
and plain-speaking sometimes go
unappreciated; lean into your intuition
this time and keep your advice to
yourself. As well-meant as they are,
there is a chance your words may
be taken as unwelcome criticism.

With Aquarius as your opposite
sign, sometimes you need to relax
your royal Leo control and submit to
the way the wind is blowing.
Now is one of those times.

The keys to success
this time will be patience
and persistence. You are
good at both of those.
Bide your time.

You are warm and compassionate,
a natural born leader, quick to nurture
the extraordinary talents and unique
value of those you surround yourself
with. Be sure they know you
appreciate them.

Your Leo love of learning and
commitment to the best-for-all goal
will ensure you fix your focus on the
task at hand. A more comprehensive
understanding will simplify
your approach.

People are drawn to you, there's no doubt about it; now it's time to make the most of your Leo talents and pull others together.

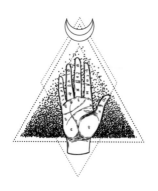

Do not shy away from this challenge. Nothing worth doing seems easy at first, but you are more than up to this one.

Your first impulse was the right one – now is not the time for second-guessing yourself. Steady your hand and go for it.

This will not be the easiest journey,
but it has your name all over it. It
might turn into a bit of a plod in parts,
but with your head down, putting one
foot in front of the other, you
will get there.

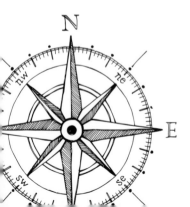

Your spontaneous nature
combines with supreme bravery,
determination and strength, making
you a true force to be reckoned with.
Decisive action is required, and you
are more than up to the task.

Self-belief is never in short
supply for you Leo, and just as well.
Your honest, pragmatic approach
won't let you down. You have the deep
knowledge already within you to
make the right choice in
this decision.

Perhaps it is time to change your approach to this one... unusual as it is, there is a very small chance you might have been a tiny bit wrong. But, you know, shake it off – it happens to everyone once in a while.

Dependable is one thing, tedious is another. Make sure this one doesn't end up being so predictable that you (or they) lose interest.

Time to let go and allow things
to be as they are. The knotty ones do
have a way of eventually working
themselves smooth again. And if they
don't, they don't. *C'est le vie*, right?

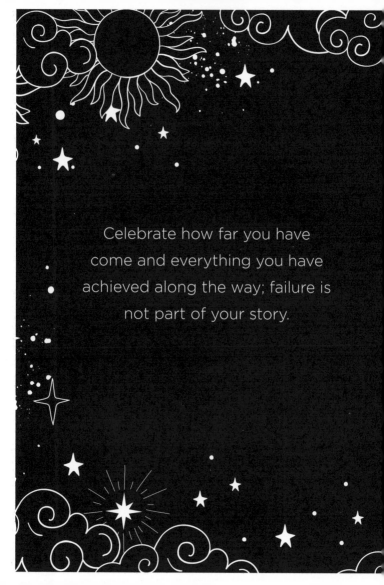

Celebrate how far you have come and everything you have achieved along the way; failure is not part of your story.

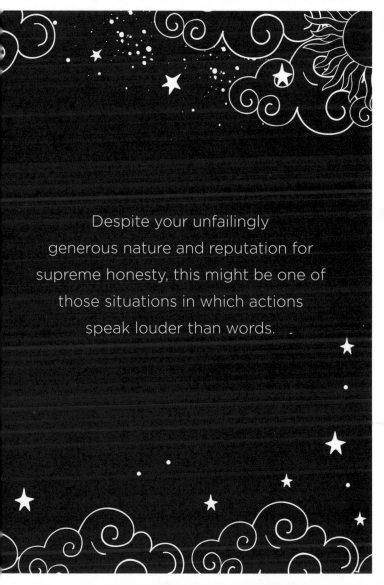

Despite your unfailingly
generous nature and reputation for
supreme honesty, this might be one of
those situations in which actions
speak louder than words.

Your need for support may be highlighted by exhaustion or some other manifestation of an inability to cope Leo. Find what you need, any way you can. Asking for help is the right thing to do; you cannot manage all by yourself.

Expressing your hopes for this situation is critical Leo; changes and adjustments may be possible, but you will need to kick it all off.

Spend some time in the sunshine to recharge your batteries and reaffirm your zing and zest.

Leave strategy and process at the door on your way in today; make a decision about the direction you are going to take and get moving.

Taking pride in your wins,
whether big or small, is key to
your life satisfaction. Time to give a
roof-rattling roar and bask in the glow
of those achievements.

It may have taken you longer
than most to decide what you want
and to sort those priorities into order.
But now you're clear, your Leo
optimism and tenacity will ensure that
no one is more likely to succeed than
you. Time to make it happen.

Usually you are so in charge
Leo, it can feel very disorienting
when things seem not to be going
your way. But trust that there is a
greater plan at work right now.
Breathe, stay in the moment, relax
your grip on that you are seeking to
hold and this too shall pass.

A different approach is required Leo. In your heart, you know that there is a better way to go about this. Don't allow yourself to be distracted from your goal.

A fire sign, and ruled by the sun as well, there is a whole lot of heat in your system Leo. But don't forget to stay cool-headed and grounded as you allow the energy to rise in you, otherwise you may burn out and it will all have been for nothing.

Time to pull back from all those commitments and spend some time basking in the warm glow of, well, yourself. Take a long, languorous stretch, turn yourself around a couple of times and settle into a warm patch of sunlight for a while.

It's all possible, especially for you Leo. But you might need to look at this one from a different angle. The direction of your approach will make all the difference.

You may need some help with this one... and others may well surprise you. Luckily, you are surrounded by adoring supporters, so make the most of it.

Get out into the fresh air
while you think this one through Leo
– you need plenty of oxygen to keep
that flame burning.

Laying down the law isn't really your leadership style Leo, but sometimes people just want to know what the rules are. Take a more even-handed, collaborative approach to working out these boundaries together, as a group.

Try this a different way. Listen, focus, notice, feel, acknowledge, stay present. It is not necessary for you to engage with your conscious thoughts right now.

It is looking like a big-picture approach might be the only way to achieve that best-for-everyone outcome you so hope for. Letting go of the reins might feel risky, but you need to rise above the detail and go with it.

It is essential that you forgive
the mistakes that have been made,
whether by you or by someone else.
Forgiving doesn't mean forgetting but
moving on is the only practical
option here.

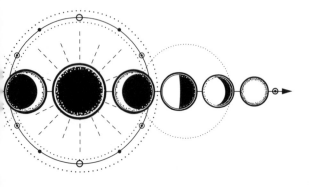

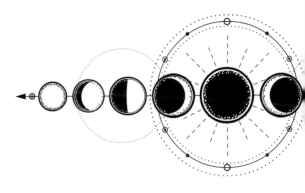

Throw that intuition into
high-gear and let it feed the flames
for you; possibility is more complex
and infinitely more beautiful than what
you can see on the surface.

You are loyal, patient, determined and the most brilliant company. But you will only keep bringing your best game if you allow your energy to replenish. Head inside for some downtime today and you'll be ready to face the world (and your fans) again in no time.

It's time to draw on the well of that famous Leo courage and steel yourself to ask the right question. Your answer will reveal itself and probably right in front of you. It has been closer than you thought this whole time.

Follow your first impression on this one; your gut instinct was correct.

You are never short of spirit,
passion and fire Leo. But the decision
to aim for a huge system-shudder of a
change is best not made on a
coin-toss. Sleep on it.

You are what you do, not what
you say. Empty words and hollow
promises are just not the way you play.
Don't be tempted to sidestep your
own integrity – it has carried you this
far in royal style.

Speaking your truth is not always a guaranteed path to cementing relationships. Suspend judgement and, if you must have your say, do consider all likely outcomes first.

Long-term pressures and projects will inevitably take a toll Leo. Ensure you are making enough time for rest, otherwise you might not be able to keep up. Reassess your position and situation as you go.

There is room enough for
both logic and emotion Leo; in
order to lead effectively, it is important
to understand that they should
stand side-by-side in the
decision-making process.

Intuition flows deep with you Leo, perhaps increasingly so. Don't write anything off at the moment – coincidences and 'strokes of luck' are all part of a more comprehensive fabric.

Visualization will be tremendously
helpful in manifesting positive results.
Spend some time mentally walking
yourself through from where you are
to the outcome you desire.

Different results represent success to different people. In this situation, it may be difficult to understand the outcome. But that's not important.

Treasure your ability to embrace
the now Leo. Going with the flow will
deliver memory-making joy that
you can reignite in the future.
Practise makes perfect.

You're a natural winner Leo, there is no doubt about it, but not all obstacles have to be dominated or beaten. So quiet that roar and see whether you might simply sidestep this one with your famous feline grace.

Be careful not to let 'dominant' tip over into 'domineering' Leo: it can be a fine line. You know what to do.

There is a difference between flattery and friendship; much as any Leo loves to bask in the warm glow of admiration, you should be wary of syrupy words right now.

Overthinking will not serve
you Leo; do not allow this one to
get under your skin.

Resist second-guessing yourself Leo
and maintain that optimistic outlook.
Your generous spirit will guide you.

When decision-deadlines are looming, but decisiveness continues to escape you, it's time to try a different way Leo. Following a cold, calm, rational approach might be difficult for such a fire-driven sun sign, but it is precisely what's required right now. Clear your head and get on with it.

Harness your determination
and call on that lion-strength Leo;
circumstances may not be quite as
they seem. Fortitude may be required.

Your success on this occasion will depend on allowing your head to rule over your heart. Make the decision clean and logical.

The path that looks familiar
is the one to follow. No map required.

If complications are starting
to dominate, press pause and
disengage, even just for a short time.
A little distance will make
all the difference.

You are an amazing people-person Leo – a warm and active listener, a supportive friend – and your intuition allows you to understand even the unsaid things. Others feel heard when they engage with you. But it is not always essential to also speak for yourself in every situation; sometimes just your presence is enough.

Both head and heart will be
required here; resist the urge to pick
a path until you are sure you have
harnessed thought and emotion
in equal measure.

Like Aries and Sagittarius, you
are ruled by the element of fire.
Warm-hearted empathy and the ability
to resolve difficult situations come
naturally to you Leo. So too does a
fondness for that spot-lit position, but
you would be best advised to learn
rather than lead this time.

As a lion, your den is important
to you... just be mindful you don't
get so comfortable in there that you
retreat for longer and longer periods.
Social interaction and frequent warm
connections are key for charging
and maintaining your
enviable energies.

Being a passionate fire sign is
all very well, but you shouldn't expect
that everyone will understand what is
truly in your heart unless you tell them.
Not all signs are created equal.

For you Leo, struggles usually serve to enhance your future strength. But that doesn't mean that you should treat adversity as a workout – conserve your power. You have plenty of it, but your reserves are not infinite.

Take the easier route this time if you can Leo, there are plenty of options. You need to keep a clear head.

Generous, lion-hearted and
easy to pick out in the crowd, you are
not often overlooked Leo. Don't let it
get under your skin if, just once in a
while, you don't feel you receive quite
the level of acknowledgement
you deserve.

Patience is a virtue and perseverance is proof of your leonine strength and the huge heart that beats within. You are blessed among the star-signs Leo, but remember that not everyone has been quite so lucky... If others seem weak and wobbly compared to you, cut them some slack.

It is never too late for an apology,
whatever its direction of travel.

The right option will soon
become clear if you simply set aside
your Leo urge to take control. There
are many players to consider.

Of course, you would be the
best choice to handle this one –
your pragmatism and intelligence are
always going to set you apart. But the
path to the finish line is not yet clear.

Relish the easy win this time; not everything is so simple. Take your rest while you are able, something much trickier, that you can really get your teeth into, is approaching.

Others may find your confidence intimidating at times, but it is just the Leo way. You don't waste time wallowing about in self-doubt, because a) what's the point and b) what even is that? Carry on in your inimitable Leo style – the world loves you.

Time to harness the best parts of your leonine nature to push through this one, rather than reactively unleashing your strength in all directions. Draw your energy upwards. Make it count.

It is imperative that you carry on, even if this wasn't part of your original plan. You need to see this one through to the end. Slowing your pace (or even worse, quitting) at this point will not guarantee the greatest rewards.

Clever, ambitious when it counts, definitely hard-working and success-driven – that's all pure Leo. But don't forget that softer, more vulnerable part; the bit that really matters. You don't have to pretend that lion's roar is the real you all the time. Open up and see what happens.

Be mindful of how your
approach might seem to others;
your success-oriented roadmap may
be interpreted as unnecessarily brutal
by some (but of course they don't
know how to tell you).

You will need to allow the
chance of chaos to ensure order
reigns, counter-intuitive as that might
seem. Throw it all up in the air and see
how it lands. Being too stubborn to try
would be the real failure here, so
don't let that happen.

Unpack that huge box of Leo talents, and spread them out to find the best combinations for new opportunities presenting themselves – you have many strings to your bow. Don't step away from a chance that seems to have been tailor-made for you.

Wisdom and truth are more
likely to turn their faces to your sun
if given some peace and solitude.
Silence and space are imperative if
you are going to recognize the
right road for this journey.

Shake off all that nervous energy, from the tips of your ears to your tail. Run, roar, swim or snore – do whatever works best for you to reset. Engage with clear intention. Stand tall and stay present in the moment.

Your squad know they can count
on you for fun, loyalty and adventure,
and they love you for it. Remember to
shine that love right back at them.

Ruled by the sun, a shy and retiring
Leo would be an unusual beast indeed.
You thrive on approval and attention,
but it is important to be mindful this
doesn't tip over into something darker,
and hungrier. Reassure yourself:
you are all that you need to be.
You are already enough.

The sun brings light, compassion,
creativity and affection into your life,
as well as opportunities for great joy.
Remember, these are gifts, and not
everyone is as lucky as you.
Be grateful.

Confidence and energy radiate from you, on a good day at least, and it is easy for others to bask in your glow. Just make sure that enough comes back to you to keep feeding that fire.

Your generosity, warmth and loyalty
are beyond reproach. Guard against
vanity, stubbornness and selfishness
– these too are within your nature,
but if you do not feed them,
they cannot grow.

This promises to be a very productive and fruitful period for you Leo, but as ever you will need to be the first one to make a move. One of your gifts is being able to see more clearly than others what needs to be done to get from A to B, and they rely on you to lead on this.

The desire to lead, and organize, is a compelling one for Leo. Take care that your self-assured confidence does not tip into a sense of entitlement.

Honesty is vital in your communications Leo, but so is allowing others to stand in their own space. Speak your piece but maintain respect and empathy for those who don't see things the same way you do.

Communication is key.
Remember to speak from the heart,
with compassion and understanding
for those you are addressing. You will
achieve better results.

There is no need to let go of
your dreams Leo, and it's certainly
not a case of settling for less. But it is
important to be clear about what you
can realistically achieve, and what the
cost of pursuing this further might be.

Usually expressive and fun to
be around, it can be a shock to others
when you reach your patience-limit
and roar like the lion you are. Console
yourself that it doesn't happen often
or without provocation.

Leo is the surest of sun signs, happiest outdoors, basking in warmth and surrounded by nature. Keep this self-knowledge in your back pocket and draw on it as your first response when you start to feel overwhelmed. Nature will recalibrate you and reset your soul.

You are a pleasure-loving sign
and adore a bit of pampering. You
work hard, but relax even harder, and
that is precisely as it should be.
Indulge yourself.

Take care of yourself Leo – a massage,
a long bath, or a special meal perhaps.
The sooner you attend to your needs
with some pampering, the better.

When things are going well, it can be
easy (and tempting) to turn your back
on the hard stuff. But Leo, that stuff is
always there, and you would be better
advised to allow and acknowledge it
alongside everything else. There is no
one without the other.

Follow your heart Leo, it is important for both your happiness and your health. Your instincts for joy and passion should not be blocked.

Planning is one thing Leo, but do not sacrifice today for tomorrow. After all, who can really say what the sunrise may bring? Carpe diem.

If a particular situation starts to feel a bit tight or uncomfortable, just switch on the full warmth of your Leo charm and you will quickly see any resistance and opposition melt away.

Be mindful that your self-confidence and loyalty don't encourage you to linger longer than you should in an unproductive or unhealthy situation; there are some things even a Leo can't fix.

Patience, lion-heart. The time is not yet right. Hold your roar and keep your energy in reserve for when you need it most.

Keep your plans adaptable and a greater number of opportunities for success will come your way. Balancing your expectations will ensure a vastly improved outcome.

It is vital you are honest with yourself and those around you, on this occasion especially; self-knowledge is never a weakness.

It is clear there is nothing more
to be gained here, being the last one
to leave will not win you any points.
Move on with your life – there is so
much more to do.

You like to enjoy the very best
Leo, and no one deserves it more than
you. But don't take luxuriating in all
that warmth and comfort so far that
you let your energy stagnate; stay
alert. Taking risks will be necessary
if you want the chance of those
big rewards.

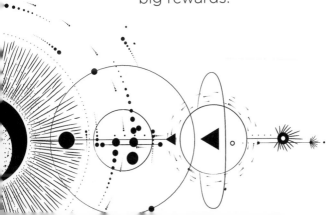

Happily comfortable and purring,
or stuck in a rut? Only you can truly
answer that question Leo. And once
you answer it truthfully, you will know
what to do... follow that knowledge.

Adopt a proactive, warm approach to resolving a misunderstanding Leo; be direct and have the courage to ask the necessary questions. Straighten things out, explain yourself, apologize if you have to.

Take care to allow others their voices, rather than assuming command too soon. Your own voice is clear and strong – essential in a Leo leader – but it can sometimes drown the opinions of others. It might take them a little longer to get to the point than it takes you.

Feedback is not always required;
true and concentrated listening is a
rare and valuable skill. Open your heart
and set preconceived notions aside.
Take the time to truly hear what
others are saying.

Investigate options in the middle-ground area. Although it looks like there are plenty of potentially exciting outcomes available to you, don't bite off more than you can chew right now.

The pressure to make too many decisions, to choose between too many options, can create a stress that leaks through into all parts of your life. Disputes and confusion are not your style – if you see them hove into view, try to take the long way round to avoid them.

Confrontation is not inevitable,
although as a fire sign you do seem to
draw the heat more often than most.
The sun will be your helper in
navigating this; maintain a steady
warmth, shine a light into those dark
corners and try your best to stay
above it all.

A clear focus on your goals
always increases your self-confidence.
Time to shine Leo.

Creativity and self-reflection are crucial components of your personal growth Leo; making time for these is vital if you are to continue to nourish yourself.

Cool the fire for a bit Leo; you need to find that balance between what you want and what you know you can get with minimum disruption.

You will not be failing if you take the decision to step away from this one Leo. It is not a question of whether you can do it or not, but rather where your energies and efforts can be most usefully invested.

If something you have been working
on still seems not to be coming
together, now is the time to walk away.
This will never come right in the way
you want it to, and even you Leo
cannot solve everything. Time to
release this and let it go, freeing
yourself in the process.

If you find yourself trying
something new, it is important to be
patient and tread carefully while you
learn the ropes Leo. This situation may
take you longer than you first
anticipated to feel comfortable with;
just take your time.

Adapting to this new normal will not happen overnight Leo, but adopting a steady approach will help you learn each of the important lessons along the way. Don't rush this process; the learning is as much the point as where you end up. Potential bonus: you may start to see yourself in a whole new (and flattering) light.

Maintaining an emotional balance in your relationships is so important Leo – sometimes people seem to be there for what they can take rather than what they bring. This can be a particular problem for you; because you seem so together, people want to be like you. Be careful not to give more than you are happy to part with.

Resist your impulse to shut down if you feel that you are suffering someone else's criticism. If you can set your ego aside, you will be able to appreciate the dialogue for what it really is: a valuable opportunity to change and grow.

Sometimes the public persona can blur the edges of the inner self a little. Now is a good time to concentrate on dusting off your personal values system and making sure that everything is aligned.

Defensiveness is simply anger and insecurity, but slightly differently branded. None of these are positives. Engage that big Leo heart and reach past the place of potential hurt; time to show them that you are truly worthy of all that trust that has been placed in you.

Do not allow the fire in your emotions to rule your responses on this one – there are plenty of paths you could take, but the wisest (and also the one that sets the best example) will require you to maintain a cool head, and a bit of distance.

Although of course you are marvellously capable in every way Leo, you cannot (and should not) expect to solve other people's life problems for them. The most you can do is hear their decisions and be supportive. Their lives are theirs to live.

Do not let your empathy
and compassion drain your own
energies Leo; it is important that you
focus on yourself for a while and
pursue your own happiness.

If a sense of security and
well-being has become more and
more familiar, all your efforts must
be starting to pay off. The journey
continues, of course, but you can
afford to pause and take
a rest for a while.

Relax and regroup Leo. Now is the time to consolidate your efforts, check in with your team and take some time for yourself before preparing for the next phase. You will be off again before you know it.

Some situations can make even our super-confident Leo anxious; when you start to feel this way, you really have to stop and take notice. Without proper planning and preparation, you will not be able to glide easily through this process, and anxiety may very well be your warning bell. Pay attention.

Do not allow emotion to
run away from logic here Leo;
there is too much at stake.

An alliance might start to feel more like a power merger Leo; with everything going so well right now, it seems there's nothing you can't do if you set your mind to it.

Guard against uncertainty and
fear Leo; your boldness is no small
part of the recipe for success. Put your
doubts to one side and take a
leap of faith.

Do not block the efforts of others
right now Leo – their frustration may
easily spill over into something else.
Instead, encourage and allow; with a
little gentle guidance events should
take the course you had hoped
for all along.

Enjoy your success and take
pride in what you have achieved Leo.
But do so with gentleness and
empathy for those who might not
have had the same outcomes.

This is not the time for
overindulging Leo, whether in
food and drink, luxury purchases
or self-congratulation.
Save it for later.

If difficulties are arising, it is important that you deal with them right away rather than storing them up for later Leo. Plenty of issues come and go; give them your attention as soon as they need it, then swiftly move on.

Flourishing and blossoming
seem to be on the cards for you at the
moment Leo, and not before time
after all that hard work you've been
putting in. Enjoy that warm glow
of contentment.

Everything seems to be settling into place for you Leo, with a new sensation of stability and security resulting. Channel some of this positivity into long-term projects and investments, so you can continue to reap the rewards further down the line.

Anything is possible for
you Leo; believe in yourself and
act on your dreams.

Your intelligence and your people-pleasing talents, as well as the fact that you genuinely enjoy being in the spotlight, all mean that this one should be an easy win for you. Do enough to get yourself across the finish line first, of course, but there is no need to humiliate the opposition. Be gracious in victory.

Take matters into your own hands Leo, the path you need to follow is yours alone to travel; no magic carriage will appear. Your dreams will not come true unless you make a conscious decision to follow them yourself.

It is important that you accept invitations and opportunities that come your way right now Leo; no excuses. Some very interesting propositions may be waiting for you... but they can only result if you make yourself available.

Keep your chin up Leo; don't let unusually difficult situations or events knock your famous confidence. Whether you are suffering through setbacks or uncertainty, there is plenty of learning in this. Your reward awaits you on the other side.

If you are feeling unusually introverted, or more extrovert than usual, go with it, Leo. Listen to what your body and your instincts are telling you.

Don't take this decision too hastily Leo... you do not yet have all the information you need to make the right choice. Think long and hard, ask advice and share your concerns with those you trust. You have several talented problem-solvers close to you; request their help.

Look carefully at the people around you Leo. If you have been experiencing frustration with the dynamic, or a lack of motivation, ask yourself how much of an impact the way you are interacting is having on everyone. Answer honestly.

Resist your need to be admired Leo,
It may lead you down an unnecessary
and unproductive path.

Even if you are not able to take a holiday at the moment Leo, devoting some time and thought to planning a special one for the (not-too-distant) future will prove to be a real tonic.

Teamwork is an important facet of your life Leo; remember that while many love to follow your lead, it is important that you allow others to shine as well. Holding the door open will only enhance your status and position, not diminish it.

A beautifully expressive confidence shines through all you do Leo... but that doesn't stop the bite when you allow too much time dwelling on others' opinions of you. This has always been a sticking point, but letting go of that which you are not able to control has never been more important than it is right now.

New contacts will bring exciting
opportunities Leo, but you will need to
be watchful and patient. No instant
gratification this time, biding your
time will reap the rewards.

Keep your eyes open to all
that is going on and try to avoid too
much focus on one thing right now
Leo. A leader like you needs to survey
a lot of ground at once, so
keep your head up.

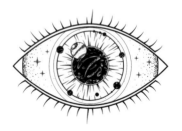

Renewed contact with old friends or colleagues could result from invitations accepted or leads followed up. Don't be too cautious about saying 'yes' right now.

Are you sensing an inexplicable frostiness or distance from a previous friend or ally at the moment Leo? It's worth spending some time reconnecting to understand what's happened here – undercurrents not of your making may be having an unwelcome effect.

Focus on the people in your life who are worthy of your time – this doesn't mean taking a judgemental approach, but rather accepting that some are too icy to be defrosted even by your famous Leo warmth. Those, you can safely let go of.

Even when your confidence levels feel lower than normal, your people-meeting skills are still markedly more polished than most. Make the most of them at the moment, no matter if you are feeling a little uncertain – your winning personality and natural warmth make an irresistible combination.

Rebalance those life-scales Leo – restore harmony by devoting some time and energy to a relationship you have been neglecting of late.

Perhaps it feels like circumstances always require you to put yourself out there, to set things up, to get the ball rolling... and maybe you're right. But, honestly, that puts you front and centre every time, and that's not such a bad place to be is it?

Set thoughts of strategy and success aside Leo. Being around the right people at the right time can be the purest pleasure, the kind that resonates strongly with you. Enjoy the pleasure of company for its own sake at the moment.

The stars line up and the sun shines for you more often than most Leo. This doesn't mean that things are always easy, or that when they are difficult they don't feel tough. But do accept and acknowledge the blessings that fate and friends have brought to your life, with humility and gratitude.

Harness your expansive energy
and clear-eyed wisdom to focus on
areas that will encourage and enhance
positive life experiences. Travel, new
connections, new hobbies, reawakened
passions – everything is possible,
so choose carefully.

Time for a life clear-out
maybe Leo? Have a mental audit
of the places and people you are
spending time and energy on at the
moment; it's important that the
balance sheet looks right to you.
If there is a deficit in one area or
another, you need to correct it.

Pushing onwards continually will take a toll Leo. Take a break and invest some time in having a look around, checking where everything is in the landscape that surrounds you. Too much single-minded focus on the path ahead will mean that you miss an awful lot – make up for lost time now.

Leo, your energy and enthusiasm are infectious; everyone wants to be on your team. Your easy grace and the way you have of making others feel good about themselves (and warm towards you) are invaluable skills right now. Wield them generously and build up that contacts list. A time is coming when it will be useful.

Spending time with friends,
away from all those demands and
expectations and responsibilities,
would be a rare and intensely
nourishing experience right now Leo.
Laughing and sharing will help release
a lot of that silent tension that's been
building up, and everything will look
brighter all of a sudden.

Stepping back into an active, make-things-happen role will be a breath of fresh air for you Leo – you may realize how much you were missing it! The group will benefit enormously from your bold and vigorous presence.

Worrying about next steps and 'what ifs' isn't going to work out for you at the moment Leo – energy spent on the negatives could be twice as effectively employed on the positives. Reframe your approach for a much stronger outcome.

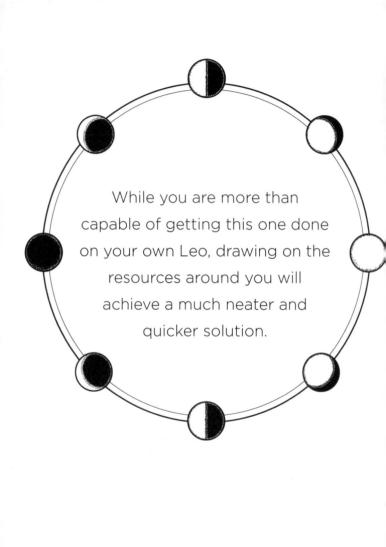

While you are more than capable of getting this one done on your own Leo, drawing on the resources around you will achieve a much neater and quicker solution.

Solving this puzzle may very
well depend on asking for help Leo.
Others have important ideas and key
knowledge to share that could be of
considerable value to you right now,
but if you don't ask you will
never know.

Targeting your friends and contacts for help and guidance is perfectly acceptable... as long as you return the favour when required. If it's all a one-way street, they might not be quite so amenable to your lion-purr next time you turn up with a request or two.

Take care of your energy right
now Leo. While you have plenty of it,
with the sun and fire both on your
side, you give so much of yourself in
everything you do that you have to be
sure to replenish your stores regularly.
Take time for yourself.

Tension is not unfamiliar to you and in fact may often spur you on to even greater successes Leo... but that doesn't mean it is a benign force. You need to acknowledge and deal with sources of tension and stress as they arrive, to avoid compounded impact later on.

Making your choice now, cleanly
in the present, rather than for a time
now past or a future not yet arrived,
will ensure the best result Leo.
Be in the moment.

Your wit, warmth and charm
mean your company is always in
demand and your popularity is
virtually assured everywhere you go
Leo. Use your influence and talent for
attention-grabbing to lay some
groundwork now; it's just fun at the
moment but it could pay serious
dividends in the future.

The sun breathes fire into your creativity bank, bringing you a seemingly endless flow of expressive talent. Do not take this for granted, but rather join forces with others (preferably those with different skill-sets to your own) to build a strong and lasting alliance.

You're not short on bravery at the best of times, but now you need to make the best use of your lion-heart. The more courageous you are in the present Leo, the less you will regret in the future.

Let your imagination set your
limits Leo, not the opinions (or envies)
of others. You have everything already
within you to make a success of this;
believe in yourself.

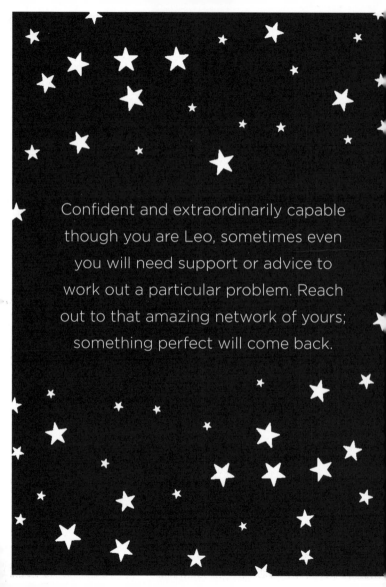

Confident and extraordinarily capable though you are Leo, sometimes even you will need support or advice to work out a particular problem. Reach out to that amazing network of yours; something perfect will come back.

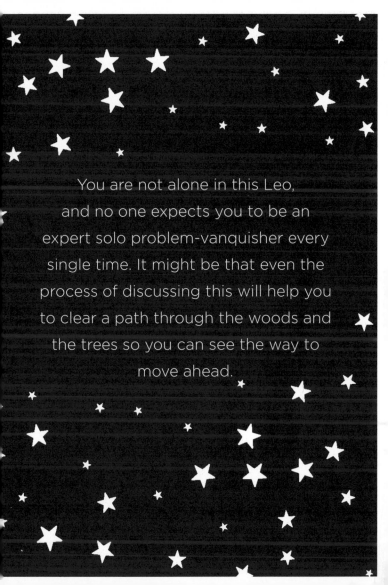

You are not alone in this Leo,
and no one expects you to be an
expert solo problem-vanquisher every
single time. It might be that even the
process of discussing this will help you
to clear a path through the woods and
the trees so you can see the way to
move ahead.

Loud and proud Leo, that's
the way of the lion. You should be
super-pleased with how things are
going, and the credit is all due to you.
Take centre stage, warm yourself in
the glow of the spotlight and soak up
the applause. You deserve it.

Your sense of self is strong right now Leo; if there is an uncertainty or insecurity whispering away in the wings perhaps it is a helpful, rather than malicious, voice, and one that you should take heed of. There are always ways to be better, and oh how you love a challenge!

The impetus must come from
you Leo... all the opportunity in the
world awaits, but you must be the one
to make that first move.

Take some time to reflect on all the little successes that are piling in right now Leo. It's worth doing a stock-check every now and then anyway, but it's also pretty good for feeding that all-important self-esteem.

Time to seal the deal Leo –
get everyone together and
sign on the line.

Focus on visualizing where you
really want to get to right now Leo.
With everything else that's going on all
around you, it's easy to be distracted
from the most important things: those
you love and the path you are
travelling together.

The world is wide open and waiting
for you, full of golden possibility – and
what a glorious feeling that is Leo.
Just be sure you pace yourself
and be sure not to burn out
before you get to the best bits.

Don't be seduced by the drama of
a particular situation Leo; although
you might very much want to
play your part in this one, you would
be well advised to simply take
your seat in the audience.

Conserving your resources is the cleanest approach right now Leo – make sure you have back-up, however that makes best sense to you, and keep plenty in reserve.

Even a golden child like you can come up against doubters occasionally Leo. If someone seems keen to steal your thunder or pinch your crown, remember that their behaviour reflects back on them rather than tarnishing your glow in any way.

Temptation is not an unfamiliar companion Leo, and though you usually bat away the little whisperings of 'maybe' or 'just this once' fairly decisively, that doesn't mean it's always easy. Keep a cool head and consider the likely repercussions. Then say 'no'.

There's a (very good) chance
that you are overstretching yourself
again Leo – never one to want to miss
a good time, burnout is only ever
another couple of late-nights away.
Do yourself a favour and spend some
time alone, in peace and quiet.

Sometimes life seems to be a constant juggle between good health and good times Leo, but you must approach this with wisdom; don't sacrifice your well-being for the empty fizz of fleeting fun.

Travelling lighter will only be possible
if you put down some of the weight
you have been carrying Leo. You can
choose what to take with you and
what to leave behind now.

Set thoughts of the past aside
Leo; it's time to clear some space
for all the beautiful new memories
you are about to make.

With the support and encouragement of the universe behind you Leo, there is nothing you cannot achieve. But the first step, as always, must be yours.

It's all very well having a plan Leo, but you need to work out the best way to execute it and, before that, whether it is actually possible. Spend a while mulling this one over, pulling it all apart and putting it back together to see what you come up with.

More research is required, but
don't get sucked down a rabbit-hole
Leo. Branch out wider instead: consult
with useful contacts, maybe even
consider calling in some expert help.

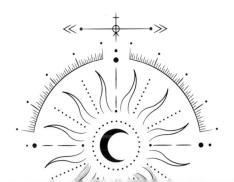

Asking for help and guidance would be a good move right now Leo – surrounding yourself with the best people gives you the greatest chance of success. Don't let your ego rule your decision-making either; if there are aspects someone else would do better, don't hesitate to hand them over.

You are not prone to paranoia
Leo, so when you feel uncertain or
suspicious of a friend's motives, pay
close attention. It might be that you
are simply insecure about the role you
play, but perhaps it is more than that.
Investigate lightly but carefully.

Don't take yourself too seriously
right now Leo; as a leader and
opinion-influencer it is essential that
you keep your own ego in check.
Remember that, as much as you know,
you are still seeing things only
from your own perspective
– everything is relative.

Release the constraints and tightness of your thinking about this issue. You are usually so dynamic and open-minded – has something gone wrong here? Whatever it is, you need to set it right and actively decide to oppose any possessiveness or urge to dominate that you might be experiencing.

The universe is on your side;
as much as you prefer the stability and
certainty of those lower-risk options,
you can certainly afford to take a leap
of faith now and again Leo.

Time to tick off those essential errands, make sure all is in order at home and that you are up to date with your chores. Settling down in your lion's den for a while is an important part of your own self-care, but first you have to make sure it's a place you want to be.

If that roar is a little rusty and your mane a bit bedraggled, it's likely time to take some rest Leo. Shutting down all that output for a while will allow your soul time to recuperate, your brain time to refresh and your creativity time to replenish. Don't rush this process – it will take as long as it takes.

Plenty of the people closest to you are used to bathing in the golden glow of reflected light, so when you turn away for a while they will notice. If your compassion-stores are running a little low right now Leo, make room for those who have something to offer in preference to those who are looking for what they can take.

Being direct rather than
simply supporting and enabling
those who enjoy listening to their own
voices is the order of the day Leo.
Resources are limited, and that
includes your patience. You have
your own life to get on with.

You are a social beast Leo, but for whatever reason you might be struggling to draw up that energy at the moment. All that juggling takes a toll sometimes. You will soon start feeling much more like yourself again.

If you are feeling open and adventurous, now is a great time to try something new in terms of physical exercise – something a bit different to your usual go-to would be best. Whatever you try, you will most likely pick it up easily and come to relish the new opportunities it brings.

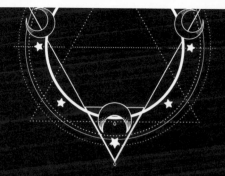

Everything looks bright for you
Leo, and the time is right to check
in with yourself about your hopes for
the next phase and how you plan to
achieve them. Time to set some
wheels in motion.

A friendship, partnership or contact will bring opportunity your way Leo; stay open-minded and receptive to the possibilities, and let your natural warmth and charm do the rest for you.

Difficult as it might be for
such a gregarious type, your plans
are best kept to yourself right now
Leo. Until they are more fully formed
and you are ready to present them to
key stakeholders, don't go shooting
your mouth off or thinking out loud.
There may well be listeners who would
be happy to claim your ideas
as their own.

Tighter planning will reap
rewards Leo, especially if you
take the time to iron out the wrinkles
and fine-tooth comb the details before
you move any closer to the action
phase. Prepare to succeed.

Not every Leo has an
earth-shattering roar, but you
do all have that expansive
determination, your lion-heart guiding
you through when it counts the most.
Make full use of your power now.

Pushing others into doing things
your way is not right Leo. Short term,
of course, it will get you what you
want. But long term it will simply
cause resentment and mistrust.

Loving vibes are strong with you Leo, only make sure you are not misreading anyone else's signals. Love comes in many different guises.

Achievement manifests in many different ways Leo; don't forget to notice and celebrate as you go.

Your intuition may lead you to
the fact that someone is keeping
something from you. Don't pressure
them, but gently encourage a situation
in which they might feel comfortable
opening up. You know what to do.

Super-productivity is strong
with you at the moment Leo, but
energy is a finite resource. Best to
tweak your priorities list so you can
be sure all the most important
things will get done.

Getting people's attention is rarely a problem for you Leo; just make sure you target that focus to say exactly what needs to be said.

Inspiring ideas and creative
vision about your next steps will
flow abundantly if only you release
the façade of control long enough
to allow some breathing room.
The universe has plenty in store
for you – trust and float.

Remember to back up your
ideas with reasoning and research.
You know your concepts are brilliant,
but others might take some
convincing. Don't allow a lack of
preparation to let you down.

Eyes are on you, as is so often
the case Leo. Make use of this
phase to build and consolidate
your connections with warmth and
positivity. Shine your inner light and
you will leave everyone glowing.

The ability to encourage others
is one of your many strengths Leo;
sometimes, even simply allowing them
to warm themselves by your fire for a
while can make all the difference. Be
generous with what has been
gifted to you.

First published in Great Britain in 2021 by
Greenfinch
An imprint of Quercus Editions Ltd
Carmelite House
50 Victoria Embankment
London EC4Y 0DZ

An Hachette UK company

A CIP catalogue record for this book is available
from the British Library

HB ISBN 978-1-52941-233-8

Every effort has been made to contact copyright holders.
However, the publishers will be glad to rectify in future editions any
inadvertent omissions brought to their attention.

Quercus Editions Ltd hereby exclude all liability to the extent
permitted by law for any errors or omissions in this book and for any loss,
damage or expense (whether direct or indirect) suffered by a third party
relying on any information contained in this book.

10 9 8 7 6 5 4 3 2 1

Designed by Ginny Zeal
Cover design by Andrew Smith
Text by Susan Kelly
All images from Shutterstock.com

Printed and bound in China

FSC
www.fsc.org

MIX
Paper from
responsible sources
FSC® C016973

Papers used by Greenfinch are from well-managed forests
and other responsible sources.